SHOW PIECES

By the same Author

FUN WITH FLOWERS

PICTURES WITH FLOWERS

MORE PICTURES WITH FLOWERS

101 IDEAS FOR FLOWER ARRANGEMENT

FIRST STEPS WITH FLOWERS

MY ROSES

FLORAL ROUNDABOUT

PARTY PIECES

FUN WITHOUT FLOWERS

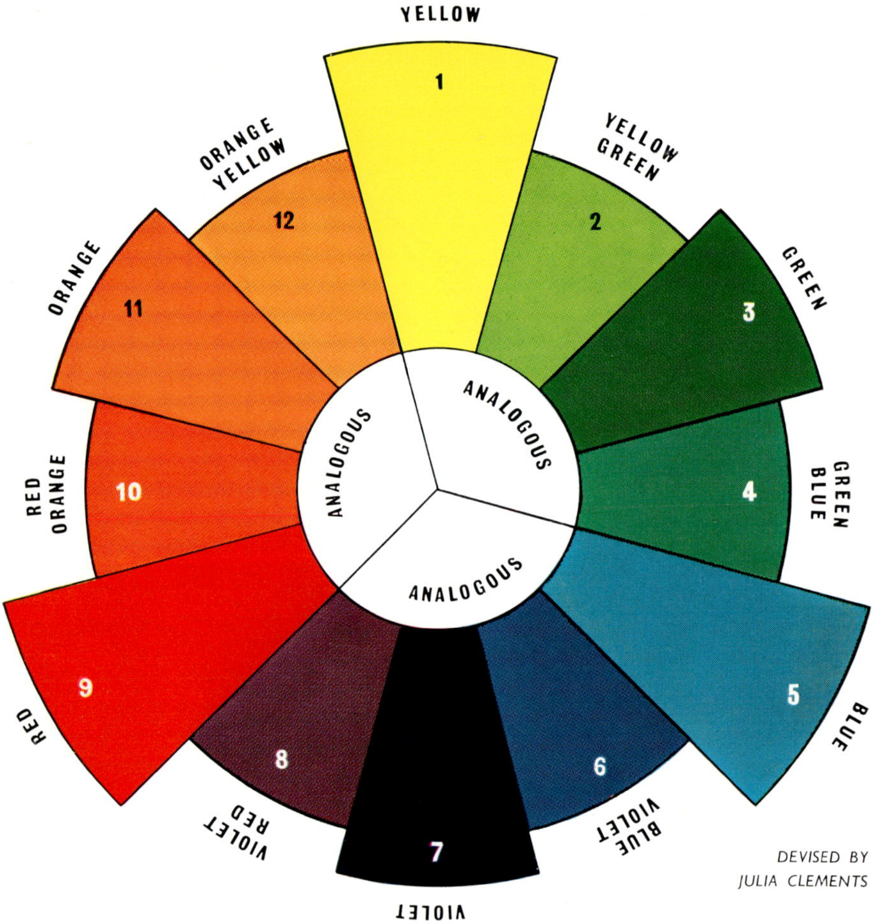

FLOWER ARRANGERS' COLOUR WHEEL

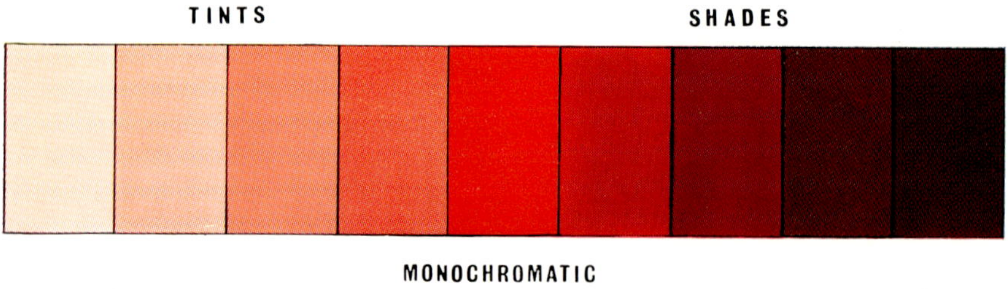

SHOW PIECES

A Handbook for Exhibitors, Organizers, Judges and Stewards at Flower Arrangement Shows

by

JULIA CLEMENTS

PEARSON · LONDON

Printed by The Vandyck Printers Limited
Bristol and London
Bound by Key & Whiting Ltd., London

Contents

1	Introduction	1
2	The Value of Shows	7
3	Show Themes and Suggestions for Classes	9
4	Preparation for Show Work	15
5	Interpretative Compositions ..	22
6	Definitions	28
7	Hints for Judges	37
8	The Work of Stewards	47
9	Invitation and Exhibition	50
10	Hints on Attracting the Public to your Show	53
11	Appendix	57
12	Prizewinning Show Designs	58

In recognition of the good work of all members of the National Association of Flower Arrangement Societies who are doing so much to spread the love and use of flowers among themselves and members of Women's Institutes, Townswomen's Guilds, Horticultural Societies and other interested organisations.

1

Introduction

THIS is a book about Flower Arrangement Shows. Although reluctant to lay down principles which in a few years time might be obsolete, I feel sure that there is a need for a book as this. For many years now I have been concerned with the organisation and judging of shows, and realise what an important part they are beginning to play in our social and cultural lives. My experience suggests that there must be some basis upon which the tens of thousands of flower arrangers can establish their work and plans for Flower Shows, which, as never before, enlighten and interest the general public.

I think it obvious that the local Flower Show has always been looked upon as part of our way of life. Fostered and inspired by the Royal Horticultural Society, established in London in 1804, almost every city, town and village in Britain organises its own flower show every summer. It is at these local shows that foreign visitors see what they so often describe as democracy working at its best, for the Lord of the Manor and the village postman meet on common ground to discuss their mutual interest in gardening. Although these shows used to concentrate on horticulture and the products of the garden, there was always a small space, often at the back of the hall or marquee, given over to entries of "bowls of flowers arranged for effect". It was here before the Second World War that many ladies, possessors of fine gardens and good gardeners, showed their skill at placing their flowers to the best effect for the home. Needless to say, such displays were usually judged by the horticultural judges, who invariably awarded the prize either to the biggest bowl or that containing the finest blooms. I seem to remember that as the same few exhibitors entered each year and nearly always got the prizes, other would-be competitors were invariably intimidated.

Now times have changed.

I remember travelling on the *Queen Elizabeth* in February 1947 on my way to the International Flower Show in New York, and discussing with the late Lord Aberconway, who was to be principal guest at the show, the future of British flower-shows in the post-war years. Later at the International Show we both stood in amazement before the illuminated niches of the flower arrangement classes, displaying what were surely works of art. Accustomed as we were in Britain to seeing large, symmetrical bowls of beautifully grown flowers shown without backgrounds, it was certainly exciting to see linear-patterned designs showing perhaps a twig, or only five flowers, which were not even grown by the exhibitor. Lord Aberconway wondered if such staged exhibits could be shown at our own Chelsea Flower Show, and many readers will remember those electrically lighted niches seen at Chelsea in 1948, in which the most beautiful exhibits were staged. These seemed even more lovely than those I had seen in the United States, because at home we were using the rare and varied plant material grown by the competitor whereas in New York the accent was on design. It became quickly evident all over the country that the "Bowl arranged for effect" was not enough for our post-war women who were hungry for some form of self-expression. Although many talks and demonstrations were given in Britain at this time in an attempt to arouse, even foster, this new need, the old Horticultural Societies seemed not to want any change, and on many occasions very strong opposition to the new ideas was expressed.

I remember in 1949 being asked by the editor of *Smallholder* if I would reply to an article entitled "Let's get rid of this Petticoat Influence", which he had just published. I did so, and readers today may be interested to read what I said then:

"As I am one who, for some years, has been pressing for the inclusion of more decorative classes in our shows, I feel I am well qualified to reply to what Mr. Smith calls the 'Petticoat Influence' on our show schedules.

"There is a new generation of amateurs who would like to become interested in horticulture and join societies, but they are being held back, intimidated by the language used and the superior knowledge of the horticulturist. To many, flower arranging is their only hope of a start.

"I do not agree with Mr. Smith, who feels it is a step backward to include so many decorative classes in our schedules. I think it is a step forward, for I am convinced that many of our future horticulturists will certainly be drawn from the ranks of those who started by arranging flowers.

"This has been proved in America, where 500,000 women now regularly practise the art of arranging flowers at their monthly garden club meetings.

"As these women become more proficient in the art, they naturally desire better and more varied material, and so their attention is turned to growing their own flowers. In other words, they become horticulturally minded through flower arranging.

"When I returned to England last year, having spent six months in the United States talking to members of garden clubs, I was astounded at the tremendous interest shown by flower lovers in

Britain who were clamouring for more knowledge about flower arranging. I could not, and still cannot, cope with the number of requests I receive to talk to audiences on this subject.

"Women, and indeed many men, need this expression of creating a picture with flowers. Their creative ability has been hampered for many years owing to restrictions in the schedules.

"Flowers are not rationed, however, nor are they wanted for export, and we in this comparatively small island have better material and of a greater variety than anywhere else in the world. Then why not give our women, and men, a chance to show what they can do?

"The people who wish to arrange flowers may not yet have good horticultural knowledge, but they are hammering at the doors of the societies in an effort to get a wider hearing.

"They want a greater variety of decorative classes, but not necessarily at the sacrifice of horticultural classes. They want to be able to display their artistic skill, and I am convinced that if Horticultural Societies do not listen to them, they will form their own Clubs, and I shall be the first to help them.

"Horticultural Societies have everything to offer, their wide knowledge could be of value to this new demand, so why not keep it in the family, instead of cutting it out as your contributor suggests?

"If I were running a Horticultural Society on business lines, I would throw open the doors to the followers of this new interest and I am sure my membership would swell, for husbands and wives could attend meetings together. I want everyone to have a chance. Wake up you Horticultural Societies and let the flower arrangers in!"

So, even then, I was convinced that flower-arranging had a great future. Apart from relieving the boredom of our post-war restrictions, this new art could open the eyes of many who had not before been aware of the beauty of growing things. At this time I was not thinking of those who lived in the country but of those in bombed cities and industrial areas who desperately needed some expression of beauty. Flower arranging had much to offer to the town- and country-woman alike, because I was convinced that anyone could arrange even a few flowers artistically, providing she followed a few simple principles of design.

Mr. Theo. Stephens, a great garden-lover who, owned and edited that unique magazine *My Garden*, staged, with his usual foresight, a Flower Arrangement Show in 1948 to prove what could be done with good backgrounds and an up-to-date schedule of classes which allowed for all tastes. It was an instant success, many of the early believers in the flower arrangement movement winning most of the first prizes. The schedule we drafted was copied in various parts of the country although it proved to be too revolutionary for many Societies. Soon, however, from all parts of Britain there came a demand from women eager to prove what they could do if they were given the chance. They had never had any influence on the settled and established ways of Horticultural Shows in the past and it soon became obvious that, in order to satisfy this need, new clubs must be formed. We sent out forms showing how this could be done, whilst other enthusiasts in various parts of the country, such as those in Dorset, Leicester, Colchester and London, started to establish new clubs and stage Shows devoted entirely to flower arrangement such as we had never seen before.

Many other enthusiasts were encouraged to start their own clubs and it is to these devoted women that so much is owed today, and it should be remembered that their interest and devotion to club work has given substantial support to many charities. Hospitals and schools have been helped too and as the many projects of these pioneers became more varied so it became obvious that the demands for guidance became too heavy for the few.

I would like to pay tribute here to all those members of the Flower Arrangement Caretaker Committee, whose efforts were eventually rewarded when one effective organisation called the National Association of Flower Arrangement Societies was formed in July 1960.

Not all of us like too many rules, but the larger an organisation becomes the greater the need for some basic principles. Although I am a born "non conformist", I'm sure we must admit that most of us have reached our best work by conforming to principles at some stage of our development. I am convinced now that the best way to help thousands of beginners is to present to them some basic principles of judging, exhibiting, stewarding, etc., and that is the reason for this book.

No book concerned with any form of artistic expression is ever complete because art is progressive, but if this book helps some of the thousands of eager exhibitors, stewards, judges, and show-organisers, then I shall be happy that I tackled it.

Chelsea 1962 JULIA CLEMENTS

2

The Value of Shows

THE whole point of any visual or social art is that as many people as possible should look at it: so that for our purpose Flower Arrangement Shows are the perfect answer.

A Flower Arrangement Show is for everyone. Whether you are a member of a Club, an exhibitor or a spectator who loves to look at beautiful things, it is a meeting ground for all who love to grow and use flowers for indoor decoration and as a means of artistic self-expression. It also provides an occasion for the exchange of ideas which will stimulate new lines of thought and it can become an oasis to which many who are tired of the rush of the world today may come for spiritual refreshment.

Shows are of particular value to new members of Clubs, while experience is gained by exhibiting, even in the novice classes, much can be learned from discussing the more advanced exhibits. At the same time the more experienced members need to compete with each other, for it is only after years of stiff competition that you will be familiar with all or most of the pitfalls, and will be able to go forward to the greater heights offered by invitation classes.

Many contend that flower arrangement, as an art, should not be competitive. On certain scores I am inclined to agree, but I am convinced that nothing which is really worth while has ever succeeded without competition. Competition is a spur, it urges us to do our best, it makes us try harder than we really need to; and even if we do not win, the effort will have helped us learn facets of the subject which perhaps we had not realised before.

It is only when all the problems of competition have been appreciated that one is fundamentally ready to exhibit non-competitively on a higher plane. Then creation rises beyond competition, as in the work of the many really fine artists we have in Britain today. In fact, opportunities must be made for this to happen; but I am sure these experts will agree that they would not have reached this stage of full expression without the initial competition.

By this I do not mean that there should be no non-competitive work until the top has been reached: on the contrary, shows are really community affairs and the many new members of Flower Arrangement Societies who are not conversant with the principles of competition are more likely to show their work locally in the non-competitive classes than they are in competition. For this reason I would urge all Show Committees to include in their schedules some classes of each, ensuring that one or more of the competitive classes for the new members are easy and uncomplicated. If encouraged at these early stages, there is every likelihood of the new members becoming the stalwart supporters of future shows. It has been found that those who *start* by doing non-competitive work are very rarely satisfied for very long, as they quickly reach a stage when they wish to know how they fare in competition with others.

All this means that everyone must be catered for, particularly as shows have educational as well as aesthetic value. Plants can be named, advice given, help proferred—in fact there is no town so big or so small that it cannot benefit from a Flower Arrangement Show. No subject will succeed unless publicly exhibited and acclaimed. So show your friends what you can do. Have a show!

3

Show Themes and Suggestions for Classes

THE problem facing most newly elected Flower Club Committees is how to make their particular show better than the rest. This *is* a problem, for in the rush of freshly kindled interest, many committees try to offer too much too soon, and find that in their enthusiasm they have exhausted all their ideas and resources at once, leaving no scope for future shows.

Of course the committees of National and Area shows should stretch to their limits each time in order to stage the most imaginative, most artistic and most educative show, for it is at these big shows that everyone congregates to be stimulated by new ideas; but my advice to most Club Show organisers is to concentrate on their locality, keeping the interests of the people around them well in mind.

There are hundreds of housewives in small communities most anxious to know how to make a simple flower arrangement. Please do cater for them, for it must be rather disconcerting for the newly initiated, on visiting a Flower Arrangement Show to be confronted with such classes as "Rippling Harmony" or "Cascading Analogous". Too many advanced classes are apt to deter the onlooker. By all means have a number of interpretative classes which will stretch the imagination and skill of the advanced members: but do include a number of simple classes, even a few free-style or non-competitive exhibits, so that the general public can be attracted by thinking "This is something I could do". Classes for any named position in the home will always attract the public, for they offer something they want to know about, e.g. "An Arrangement for an Entrance Hall", or "For the Sideboard", or "For the Window Sill". An arrangement of "My Own Choice" for first year members or an arrangement using a candlestick, a bottle, a wine-glass or a jug are others which might immediately solve the problem of many would-be competitors. Again, an arrangement of wild flowers, or one using three flowers, will help them to appreciate that flower arranging need not take up a lot of time or money.

Of course these very people we aim to attract in the beginning often become very quickly proficient themselves, and need further classes to stimulate their interest. And that is why I advocate a mixture of both, for one is then catering for the advanced at the same time as encouraging the new.

To accent a particular locality, you could have classes featuring scenes like the Sussex Downs, the Welsh hills, or even the local High Street—just imagine what colour could be represented here with ideas of fruit designs for the vegetable shop, flowers in picture-frames for the art shop, flowers in antique containers for the antique or junk shop, flowers in a shopping basket for the grocer's and so on. All of these ideas will cause comment in the locality and bring your show to the notice of many who might not have been previously attracted. But do tell them about it. Ask each tradesman to display a bill stating his shop is to be represented.

Other ideas for young clubs could be classes featuring the seasons, e.g. "Summer Garden", or "Summer's Roses", "Burst of Spring", "Autumn Glory" or Winter's Tale". Classes featuring special containers, such as pewter, pottery, jug, basket, or wood are all easy items; even an arrangement based on an accessory will have as much appeal as arrangements accenting a certain variety of flowers.

Try a class to interpret the weather: just imagine how many different exhibits could be displayed under "Bright and Sunny", "Misty" or "Windy". "Dull and Cloudy" could be another, whilst "Rain", "Heat", "Fog", "Calm" and "Gales" would all draw interesting designs. Another class could be one to illustrate magazine titles, such as *Vogue*, *Men Only*, *Flair*, *Home*, *Do It Yourself*, or others. A class for British Industries could well be interpreted, as well as a number some of us have seen already, such as an arrangement of flowers incorporating glass, candles, china or fabric. Many of us have either judged or shown in classes such as the interpretation of book titles, song titles, quotations, jewels, moods, trades, or professions, all of which will attract the public, who love to work things out for themselves. But do remember that since flower arrangement is what we might call the end-product of gardening, flowers and other plant material should predominate in all exhibits. In fact interest is always aroused by classes featuring one of the varieties of flowers in season, such as daffodils, lilies, delphiniums, sweet peas, irises, roses, gladioli, dahlias and chrysanthemums. To make the exercise more complete state the *type* of arrangements you want shown, such as *Modern* Arrangements of Irises", "*Formal* Arrangements of Sweet Peas", and add the words "any foliage or any other plant material may be used".

An overall title or theme will often attract attention to more important shows, or shows held in the midst of busy cities or towns where it might be difficult to arouse local interest. In the U.S.A. I once visited a show entitled *Through Pink to Purple* in which every exhibit was made in flowers, leaves and other plant material in colours of pink, mauve, crimson, pale purple, and violet. "Pink Champagne" could be one class in which pink flowers are placed in a champagne glass; "Purple Interlude" could be another; "In a Crimson Container" could be another, and so on. If the bills were printed in pink or purple and the stage draped accordingly you can visualise that such a show, even if staged in other colour variations, could become the talk of the town. Why not stage a show entitled *Round the World with Flowers* showing arrangements featuring different countries, or why not attract visitors by stating on your posters that you invite them to attend a Flower Arrangement Show entitled *A Wedding in Dorset* or any other county or town? Classes under this main theme heading could be: 1, "The Stag Party" (for Men Only); 2, "The Bridesmaids" (arrangements in blue or pink); 3, "The Bride" (all white arrangements); 4, "The Reception" (buffet table arrangements); 5, "The Presents" (arrangements made in all kinds of containers which could be presents); 6, "The Honeymoon" (arrangement depicting various countries or environs where the honeymoon might be spent); 7, "The New Home" (arrangements suitable for any spot in the home).

Another theme could be *Come into our Garden*, the separate classes being: 1, "The Herbaceous Border" (an arrangement featuring perennial flowers); 2, "The Rose Arbour" (an arrangement featuring roses); 3, "The Water Garden" (an arrangement in which water plays an important part); 4, "The Vegetable Garden" (an arrangement of fruits and vegetables—obviously not to include exotic or imported fruits since the title is come into *our* garden); 5, "The Shrubbery" (an arrangement showing the use of shrubs and leaves); 6, "Grown from Seed" (an arrangement featuring annual flowers); 7, "The Greenhouse" (an arrangement featuring exotic plants); 8, "Rock Garden" (an arrangement using succulent twigs and stones).

When drawing up a schedule it is as well to remember the time of the year, your locality and the ability of your members. For instance it is not advisable to include in your Spring Show a class for "All Foliage" just because you enjoyed the one you saw last summer. Remember there is little foliage about in the spring. Similarly, a class for variations of one colour is not suitable for a Christmas show. Although a number of ideas can be picked up from other shows here are a few, arranged in seasons, which might prove of help:

SPRING

"Time of Promise"
"From the Woods"
"My Favourite Container"
"Oriental Beauty" (using shallow dish)
"Modern design featuring blossom sprays"
"Time to Economise"
"Drifting Daffodils"
"Out of the Bottle"
"One on a Tray"
"Spring Quotation"
"Small flowers in a wineglass"
"Simplicity".

SUMMER

"Fascinating Foliage"
"Colour from the Garden"
"From the Kitchen Garden" (vegetables and fruit)
"As I like it"
"Holiday Memories"
"Hot Summer Day Arrangement"
"The Water Garden"
"White Wedding Arrangement"
"Buffet Arrangement"
"Pedestal Elegance"
"Variations on One Colour"
"Depicting a country".

AUTUMN

"Hedgerow Beauty"
"Harvest Home"
"In a Metal Container"
"Dare to be Different"
"November 5th"
"Blithe Spirits" (dried arrangement)
"Autumn Glory"
"Suggested by a figurine"
"Hallowe'en"
"Fruits of the Earth"
"Dahlia Delight"
"Treasures from Land or Sea".

CHRISTMAS

"By Candlelight"
(using one or more candles)
"Pantomime Time"
"Christmas Cards"
"The Holly and the Ivy"
"For the Sideboard"
(flowers and fruit)
"Festive Walls"
(swags, garlands and plaques)
"O Holy Night"
"Red and gold"
"Cinderella"
(an arrangement of greenery, fruit and vegetables using kitchen container)
"Party Time—The Glitter and the Gold"
"An Arrangement on a Christmas Wrapped Parcel"
"A White Christmas".

In all cases, do remember to state the size of the niche; whether the design is to be modern, formal, a composition or otherwise; and whether you require certain containers to be featured, as well as mentioning the plant material you wish used. An example at an Autumn show could be "Hedgerow Beauty"—(a modern arrangement on a wooden slab base featuring leaves, berries, seedheads and other plant material—not flowers—which is found in the hedgerows). Size of niche 2′ 6″ square. No accessories or drapes.

The Schedule Committee performs an important task: and do remember that more heads are better than one when the schedule is being compiled, for on it the success of the show rests.

4

Preparation for Show Work

Most Flower Club members need an outward expression for their creativeness, so there is rarely any shortage of exhibitors at shows. Of course, it is generally recognised that all members should support the work of their clubs during show time, for having enjoyed monthly meetings throughout the year, it is now their turn to support the committee, exhibiting to fellow members and public alike.

This chapter deals mainly with the preparation for the show and the conditioning of plant material, but I feel I should add a few further reminders. Before entering, *read the schedule carefully*. Read it thoroughly. As a rule a lot of thought and work has gone into its production in order to make it interesting to you and to the public it tries to attract. If there are items you do not understand, write to the secretary at once. I receive hundreds of letters each year, even some from abroad, asking me if I would clarify certain statements in their schedule. Only those who compose the schedule can give the answer, so do write to them and make sure you are clear about what is needed of you. If you think there is some ambiguous wording which might be interpreted by the judges in another way than yours, do not worry: just as you will have checked with the committee, so also will the judges, who on discovering the misleading words will either write to the secretary or confer with her on arrival. So if you clarify the position with your local secretary and all others play their part accordingly, all should be well. The problem can then be better resolved the next year.

Choose to enter only those classes you feel confident of being able to complete and do not choose too many, unless you are very experienced and have already been able to gauge the time needed to complete them all. Your best work will evolve if you have time on your hands, whereas if you are trying to complete a number of arrangements and working with one eye on the clock, your work is sure to become a little mechanical.

Make sure you have all the *equipment* you wil' need. It seems almost unnecessary to add this; and yet I recall an agonised moment for a competitor in one of the big northern shows who discovered she was short of one pin-holder which she badly needed for a modern design of chrysanthemums. No one had an extra one and no shops were open, but after thinking of all kinds of substitutes, none of which would work, I thought of the horticultural tent where the vegetables were being staged and there obtained a large potato for her. This was cut lengthwise to lie flat on the dish and holes were made in it with a pencil, allowing the competitor to insert her flowers and complete her design, which delighted the judges sufficiently to win it the second prize. *But*, it was a harrassing time for all, and there might not have been a horticultural tent nearby. So do check on all your needs, taking extras in case of accidents. Items necessary may include pin-holders, wire netting, reel wire, conical tin tubes (for mass or pedestal groups), glass orchid tubes (for short flowers high in a design), modelling clay, rubber rings (to avoid holders and fruit from slipping), twistems (to steady heavy branches at the back of tall containers), flower scissors, mist spray to moisten the surrounds of your exhibit, toothpicks (for fruit) and a long-spouted water can.

Chrysal powder (to keep flowers living longer), Sellotape, drawing pins or paper clips or stapling gun (for drapes), boxes (on which to stand exhibits for extra lift), and Mosette or Florapak (if you use it). Pieces of strip lead may be needed to hang on the wire at the back if your arrangement is inclined to tilt forward, though it should not do this if properly constructed. Also take a bucket for water and of course the necessary containers, bases, backgrounds (which should be wrapped round newspaper or on a roller to avoid creases) and accessories, to which will be added, on the day, all the flowers and plant material.

Plan your arrangements well in advance. You cannot always decide upon the flowers you might use, for the weather and market fluctuations will have to be considered; but you can make a rough sketch of the sizes and shapes of flowers you will need to enable you to create the design you have decided upon. Next the *container*. If the height of the background niche is to be three feet, to achieve good scaling you will need to make your arrangement about 2 feet 9 inches high, including container. This would allow for your vase, if an upright one is used, to be 12 inches high or slightly more; therefore if your chosen vase is shorter than this you might need a block or base or even a tin or box on which your arrangement can be stood. These items can either be specially made, painted to match the container, or covered with a swirl of material. If placed underneath your container this material acts as a base which in judging is considered as part of the arrangement and not an accessory, as back drapes are. If you are using a shallow container then you should choose plant material that will give you the necessary height of 2 feet 9 inches to fill the prescribed niche of three feet. The colour and texture of your container should be chosen with care.

Drapes. Do check if these are allowed, and if you choose to use them study the effect of their colour and texture, for both will effect your arrangement. If your arrangement is mostly shaded, use a tinted background to throw it into greater relief; on the other hand, if you have made your design using mainly light coloured plant material, add a shaded background so that the highlights will be noticed. Similarly the overall effects of your design can be enhanced by using certain textures of material. For instance a shiny surfaced drape is often better placed with dull surfaced plant material, whilst linen, rep and other dull surfaced backgrounds will give stability to arrangements of lighter textured flowers. Wild flower arrangement, those featuring fruits, and others of country atmosphere require backgrounds of coarse material, such as hessian, hopsack and other heavy weaves, but in the main follow the principle of light behind dark and dark behind light. If you make an autumn arrangement featuring wheat, beige-coloured chrysanthemums with yellowing leaves and gourds or quinces, composing this with a background of natural coloured hessian, the outline of your arrangement will be lost; whereas a brown (I think I would use a cinnamon brown) would place the complete design in stronger silhouette.

Avoid patterned backgrounds, for unless you are keeping to one colour scheme, such as pure white flowers in front of a green and white and gold embossed back drape, the patterned drape might confuse with the flowers in front of it. Net, as a background, is almost too sheer of texture to be of any value, except perhaps when used in compositions illustrating champagne, ballet, or other such themes. The vast subject of the use of drapes is interesting, for sometimes the best use of a background can be the judge's deciding factor between two equally good arrangements. The colour and texture of woven material bases is equally important. I recall a most beautiful arrangement of maroon and mauve flowers with maroon-coloured *Prunus pissardii* and reddish purple *Begonia rex* leaves. All of this was in a dull pewter container standing on a grey material base. As I analysed the design I could find no fault with it, yet I could not at once discover why it had not struck me more forcibly at first sight. I took it apart point by point and tried to discover some note of distinction, without success. I was concerned, for it was quite one of the most lovely arrangements I had seen for a long time. After more consideration I finally concluded that had the material base been of a pale mauve or lime green, even shiny crimson colouring, the design would have been lifted right out of its monotone bracket into one which could not have been resisted. The complementary to reddish purple is yellow green, and since the reddish purple in the arrangement was shaded, it would have been better to use a tinted yellow green for the base or, if wishing to keep to shades, a shiny crimson.

Bases. Bases can be made of a number of materials (see definitions, Chapter 6) and if used correctly can often help establish the balance of a design. Sometimes when a thin-stemmed plinth-like vase is used, the mass of flowers above it gives an overbalanced effect. Balance can be restored by standing the vase on a base, making sure, in good show work, that the base is in keeping with the vase and flowers above it. An oblong base will often aid a tall vertical arrangement: a tall thin design placed in a prescribed niche might leave the niche half empty, whereas if it were placed on a base the setting would become more complete, since the base is judged with the arrangement. These are all possibilities and there are no static rules, but a good experienced judge will notice these subtleties, especially in first class show work.

Accessories. These items are discussed in the chapter on compositions so whether you take them to the show or not depends upon the classes you have decided to enter. They should however be kept within the spirit of the exhibit and be of correct size, colour and texture.

Plant Material. There are many methods of getting your plant material to the show ground or hall, depending upon the length and method of your journey. However, after conditioning your flowers and other plants, it has been found excellent for long journeys to pack everything in a plastic lined flower box rather close together to avoid moving about, and tissue paper can be slid around precious blooms. Place long leaves at the bottom, followed by tall flowers, shorter flowers being placed near the ends of the others together with any shorter leaves, and special ones can be packed in a plastic bag. Cover the box with more plastic sheeting and tie it down. Place the flowers in a bucket of water on arrival at Show hall and allow them a deep drink. Another method, better for shorter car journeys, is to place most flowers in a polythene bucket containing a little water, then pull a plastic bag over the head of the blooms, tying this down firmly to the bucket to avoid loss of moisture. Fill the bucket with water on arrival to allow for a long deep drink.

Conditioning of Cut Plant Material. Much has been written on prolonging the life of cut flowers and much of it is merely confusing, for long passages on temperatures and the effect of certain chemicals are mainly intended to apply to commercial growers. Folk lore has also conveyed to us the advantages of using such ingredients as vinegar, peppermint, wine, acid, tea, copper pennies and aspirins, but few of us connected with show work and dealing with mixed flowers would have time to work out what ingredient goes with which flowers, however it proved effective. Nevertheless, a great deal of help can be given to flowers by proper conditioning, and I have found certain flower preservatives now on the market very helpful, except in the case of flowers which ooze a sticky substance, such as daffodils.

Here are some hints which I have found very useful:

1. Pick flowers and leaves late at night or early in the morning when transpiration is at its lowest.
2. Pick most flowers in bud, re-cutting their stems under water, leaving them in deep water to condition. They can be moved from light to dark, and warm to cool places to aid or retard their opening.
3. Submerge all leafy shrubs in water overnight. Split stem ends.
4. Split stem ends of all woody plant material before placing in the vase.
5. Foliage should be cleaned of dust and all damaged leaves removed.
6. Submerge in water for at least two hours, more if possible, most flat surfaced leaves, including *Begonia rex*.
7. Some glossy surfaced leaves, such as camellia and laurel, can be rubbed clean with an oily rag, but do not allow any oil to show.
8. Branches can be trimmed to shape, but obvious cuts should be disguised with water colour paints or rubbed with another branch.

5

Interpretative Compositions

LET us admit that the exhibits that often draw the most comment from members and visitors alike are those to be seen in interpretative composition classes. Yet many newcomers to the art of flower arrangement are mystified as to what exactly constitutes a composition and what makes it interpretative.

A composition is the grouping together of certain items to make a pleasing overall picture. Without perhaps realising it, you "compose" the items of furniture in a room; you also "compose" the setting of a table or the items on a mantelshelf, placing perhaps a tall vase or candlestick on each side of a mirror or clock in the centre. If you place both candlesticks on one side, leaving the other side bare, the composition on the mantelshelf would appear unbalanced. So in flower arrangement composition work, you are aiming to compose a number of items, including the flowers, into a harmonious whole to fit the space stated in the schedule. Your items may be one flower arrangement with back drape and two accessories, but in order to compose these items harmoniously the eye should be able to travel from one item to another without any jarring. Hence the reason for an appreciation of rhythm (see Definitions).

To interpret, you must have a theme in your mind first.

As a rule, the schedule will give you the initial

overall idea, which in turn should stimulate your own thoughts, and if you find it difficult to make a start, I would suggest that you write down on paper all the things that come to your mind as you think of the title of the class. Let us imagine that you have decided that you would like to enter the class entitled "Book Titles". Sit down and think about all the books you have read or known, and at the same time visualise all the plant material which might be incorporated to help you illustrate the meaning of the book. I emphasise thinking of the plant material early, for this should predominate in the final picture, and it would be useless dreaming of all the things you could include in your composition which might interpret shall we say "The Corn is Green", if the show is at a time of year when you cannot obtain corn. Of course there may be other more subtle ways of interpreting such a theme but I am writing more of the obvious at this stage.

Having decided upon the title of the book you wish to interpret, you must gather together, even if it is done mentally, all the items you *could* include which will help illustrate your point. It may be that the colour of your flowers will help, perhaps the container or the background will add to your interpretation. You may have just the right china figurine to add as an accessory, or a book, a statue, a pipe. Once you start thinking, many items will crowd into your mind and you will begin to wonder how you will compose them.

Do remember that only one of these items can become the focal interest, the others should lead to and from it, or at least be placed so that they are subservient to the main object of interest. Let us imagine that at a Christmas show you have chosen Shakespeare's *A Winter's Tale*. You have perhaps chosen this because you have a small statue portraying Shakespeare sitting in a chair reading and also because you thought that bare branches would be easy to obtain and appropriate for the winter. You begin to visualise how you will compose this and decide upon a tall branch that will fit into the three foot high niche. You then decide to whiten the branch with plaster powder to give it a more wintry effect, and finally in order to give width low down to this tall bare branch, you decide to place it in a long base or dish which you might whiten.

Yes, the idea is coming and you can hardly wait to do it. You imagine you could include a book of Shakespeare's verses opened at the appropriate page; and you have some large pine cones which if whitened would add to the effect. You also have some greenery, some spectacles for reading the book (you think) and a host of other things. Stop! Now is the time to decide which one of these items is going to be placed at the foot of your tallest point to become the focal interest, and to which all other items will lead. Shall it be the book, the cones, or the statue? Perhaps you decide to place the open book at the base of the branch and the statue slightly to the left. This I would say divides the interest and is not so good, and in addition I think the open book would become too dominant.

On thinking the matter over I feel a better way of handling this would be to place the tall whitened branch on the whitened base and insert some tallish green pine sprays for transition, then at the base of the branch I would stand the whitish model of Shakespeare and make this your main interest. A few small cones could be placed around the base of the statue and in which some small pieces of green pine could be interspersed, for otherwise the white statue on the white base would not be thrown forward sufficiently enough. Then, should you wish to emphasise your meaning by adding the opened book, it could be placed *behind* the branch in the niche, so that it is only half seen. This makes it less obvious and adds a third dimension, and it could even be stood on a further pile of books to make it higher, but at least in this way you will have concentrated your main interests in one spot (i.e. around the base of the tall stem) and the onlooker's eye will be able to travel down from the top tip of the branch on to the greenery for transition, then to the figure for emphasis; then drifting off again with low trails of greenery which completed the rhythmic movement of the whole design. In other words you have made a rhythmic composition properly scaled to fit the niche, which illustrates your meaning and which, because it is not too cluttered, will attract the judge's eye.

This brings me to emphasise the fact that all interpretative work must "speak". It must tell its story to the judge, for the judge's reaction will depend a lot upon whether the exhibit is quickly recognisable. A title may be added to help illustrate the meaning of your composition.

Thus the main points to consider in an interpretative composition are that it should have appropriate height and width, dominant interest, rhythm and balance, appropriate colouring and a third dimension, and that everything, including the accessories, should be suitably related. An accessory placed at the back of a niche is made to appear smaller and less obvious, one placed forward will seem to increase its size. Items recessed will give depth, whilst fine items placed protruding will add highlights.

Once a start has been made on interpretative work, it becomes a deep and abiding interest, often being carried into the home. It stirs the imagination of all who see it, provoking others into trying it themselves. The organisers of art exhibitions have often expressed surprise at the great numbers that flock into flower arrangement exhibitions, whereas only relatively few find their way to other exhibitions. It is because anyone can do it. Anyone can obtain a few flowers which, with a little imagination combined with an accessory, can make a picture.

I wonder how many recall the Coronation Flower Arrangement Exhibition in London in 1953 which included an interpretative class representing the countries of the Commonwealth? Fearing that these ideas were too advanced at the early stage of the progress of our clubs, I was invited to give an explanatory talk to the exhibitors. I found that to interpret a country of the Commonwealth appeared too difficult, so I threw the meeting open and asked exhibitors to answer what came into their minds when I called out a particular country. "Jamaica", I excitedly cried, and the answer after some hesitation came back "bananas", "coloured cottons and coloured people". Good, a start had been made, "Please", I then went on, "will someone do an arrangement of bananas perched perhaps on the head of a statuette of a coloured woman? Add a check cloth, if you like, but do it!". It was fun, we went on to Australia with coral and shells; to Guernsey with fruit and vegetables; to India with red flowers, saris as background and perhaps a black ebony elephant. We went to Ceylon with pool and lotus flowers, to South Africa with proteas and exotics. In fact so fast were the ideas coming that in the end we wished for more countries. The show was a huge success, thirty-eight countries were represented, and we all thoroughly enjoyed it. In fact it was getting the start that was so difficult.

When interpreting items such as metals, fabrics and jewels, colour and texture is very important. For instance, sapphire is glittering and sheer, whereas as jade is heavy and opaque. The former could be illustrated with delphiniums or other fine blue flowers in a blue glass container, whilst green succulents could be incorporated with an opaque container for the latter and perhaps a jade ornament or one carved from a piece of green soap.

Almost all classes which bear a title are interpretative. For instance, if you enter a class for a table design for a special occasion and you decide to make *your* special occasion your son's 16th birthday party, it would be much more interpretative of the occasion if you made a flower design in school colours, or used a tankard or pop bottle as a container. You might be a person who loves pink and blue flowers, and you decide to arrange these on one of your lovely lace cloths, but in interpretative work you must submerge your own likings and do something appropriate for the occasion, or else make the occasion fit your own tastes by, in this case, naming your table "Teatime with me". In an interpretative class for "Moods" you might choose "Happy" or "Doldrums", "In the Blue", "Gay" or "Jealous". Just imagine the great variety of colour and textures and accessories which could be brought into play.

Then, endless ideas could be used in a class which asked for the interpretation of a quotation. Think first of its meaning, then of the flowers and other plant material, their colour, size or shape, which will help express this meaning.

I wonder how many readers remember the array of 32 interpretative exhibits featuring Shakespearean quotations which were shown at the charity show in aid of the G.R.B.S. in 1953.

One in particular remains vividly in my mind. It was composed of a gnarled bare branch, rising from a shallow dish filled with moss and fungus, surrounded by a swirl of grey net rising high at the back. The quotation was:

> I saw old autumn, in the misty morn,
> Stand shadowless, like silence listening to silence ;

and as you gazed at it and read you felt you had to creep away in case you spoiled the silence. Yes, interpretative work is fascinating and it is also very rewarding, for most competitors find that the mind is widened and extended in searching libraries, museums and other places for facts.

6

Definitions

Most newcomers to show work find it rather difficult to understand the meaning of certain words, phrases and regulations that are so often included in the making of a schedule.

I am in full sympathy, for I often ask myself whether it matters if a bulrush is called a flower or not, as long as it appears just right for the arrangement which is being made. On the other hand I know only too well that in order for the great numbers of enthusiasts now practising show work to bring some basic understanding to the subject, there must be some method of defining these working phrases.

It is hoped, as we progress, that the schedule makers, especially those of newer clubs, will become more experienced and not lay too many unintended traps for the competitors; but in order to help those who wish for some clarification of the terms in use today, I print in alphabetical order a list which is in general use. That some will outlive their use or others be added in time, I have no doubt.

Arrangement means the artistic use of plant material unless otherwise stated in any stated or unstated container with or without a base.

Annual. A flower or a plant that completes its cycle of growth in one year.

Accessory. Any item such as a plate, ornament, book, back drape, etc., and any secondary placement of plant material which is used in addition to the main flower arrangement. Stones, shells, marbles and similar non-plant material are considered to be accessories *unless otherwise stated* in the schedule. When accessories are used the exhibit becomes a composition.

Advancing colours. Those which come in the range from yellow to red. (See frontispiece).

Analogous colours. Those which lie next to each other on the colour wheel (see frontispiece). Usually means colours of the intermediaries from one colour to the next and not beyond. To include only one primary.

Artificial. Artificial, plastic or dyed flowers are not allowed in competitions unless stated.

Balance. Can be asymmetrical or symmetrical, but should portray equality each side of the axis, focal point or imaginary central line.

Basket. A basket could have a handle or lid and should be made of any natural woven material unless otherwise stated.

Best in show. This is an award given to the best of all the first prize-winning exhibits.

Bloom. One flower or opened bud borne on a single stem, e.g. carnation, dahlia, tulip, scabious.

Biennial. Describes a flower or plant which normally completes its growth in two years.

Bowl. A bowl is a receptacle having a wide opening, the top diameter of which is greater than or equal to the height. It must rest on the table or be raised by a base not more than one third its own height. Unless otherwise stated, it is assumed that a bowl shall be viewed from all sides.

Bud. An unopened bloom not showing colour.

Base. An item on which a container can be stood, e.g. wood, metal, fabric, china, plastic, slate.

Bulrush. Whether it is a flower-head or a seed-head depends upon the stage it has reached when it is used. When tight it is usually termed a flower.

Candle is considered an accessory, unless otherwise stated. Often used for colour and height in certain designs.

Container. A receptacle in which flowers are exhibited. Can be made of any material, be of any texture, colour, shape, or design which will enhance the beauty of the plant material arranged therein.

Composition. One or more flower or plant material arrangements, used with one or more accessories and drapes if desired.

Catkins. Hazel catkins are collections of the male flower of the catkin.

Colour. Colour as it should be used, to interpret adequately the meaning of the class (see page 40). Leaves should harmonise. Stems and stamen colours are ignored. (See also Tint, Shade, Variation).

Cluster. Several fruits, berries or flowers growing close together on one stem, e.g. currants, tomatoes, grapes, phlox and climbing roses.

Condition means the actual quality of the plant material at time of judging.

Cool colours. Those which come in the range from green to blue. (See frontispiece).

Contrast. A set of two things juxtaposed to accentuate their differences. To show a striking difference by comparison.

Complementary. Something which serves to complete. The lid of a container or a tray, for instance, is complementary to the whole.

Complementary colours are those found opposite to each other on the colour wheel, i.e. they are direct completions, such as Nos. 1 and 7, etc.

Contemporary. Existing as of today.

Design. An overall plan which is made pleasing by the combination of all items used. Includes balance, rhythm and scale.

Drape. A piece of fabric or other material used behind an arrangement to give height, colour or accent, or used in niche to emphasise the spirit of the exhibit. A drape is termed an accessory and is therefore mainly used in compositions, unless otherwise stated, e.g. on occasion where no niches are provided. Small pieces of material placed *under* an arrangement are termed "bases".

Dried plant material. This may include any natural dried, preserved, pressed or skeletonised plant material; also dried fruits, seed-heads, nuts, cones, grasses or sedges, in fact anything which at the time of use is not living. Generally this does not permit painting or dyeing or the use of artificial material.

Driftwood. This is a wide term but covers wood which has been weathered by any of the natural elements, i.e. air, earth, fire or water, or that which is dead, dried, stripped, sandblasted or polished.

Distinction. Something above the ordinary yet not bizarre notable for creative use of plant material. (See page 42, chapter on Hints for Judges).

Dominant in flower arrangement means something eye-catching—something strong, influential, outstanding, overlooking other items.

Exhibit means an entry placed in a Flower Arrangement Show. It need not be in competition.

Exotic in plants, used to mean introduced from hot countries abroad and nurtured in Britain in greenhouses. Many now grow happily outside, but the term "exotic" generally refers to greenhouse plant material, and not outdoor-grown garden material.

Floral is used to cover arrangements including all kinds of vegetable matter.

Floret. A singly formed flower which goes to make up a spike, as found on delphiniums, gladioli, acanthus, phlox, lilac, etc.

Flowers. When a class refers to the use of a certain number of flowers it means blooms or opened buds borne on a single stem, such as carnations, dahlias, tulips. A gladiolus is a spike.

Focal point refers to the heart of interest in a design. The point where all stems unite, usually found at the base of the tallest or main stems.

Foliage. The leafage of a plant. Succulents and some bracts come under this heading—also stems bearing leaves. A class for "all foliage" can be of any colour.

Forced. This refers to plants brought forward, often under heated glass, to produce blooms out of season.

Formal. Usually means a conventional arrangement, which is regular and symmetrical, in a suitable container.

Fragrance. A quantity of odour which can be appreciated. Used in some classes, particularly those for the blind.

Fruit in horticultural terms usually means the nuts berries, seed-heads, gourds and cones of fruiting plants. Generally whatever develops from a flower is a fruit. In Flower Arrangement Shows also includes edible fruits such as apples, pears, cherries, bananas and grapes etc.

Genus. Botanically this means a classified group of plants such as dianthus which contains all pinks, or the genus antirrhinum which includes all species of such flowers. Plural of genus is genera.

Grasses. Since few can distinguish when grass is in seed or flower the term "grasses can be included" is added to schedules if they are needed, unless "any plant material" is stated, which of course would include grass.

Green. An "All Green" class allows the use of any green plant material—i.e. foliage, fruit and flowers etc. But it must all be green, not variegated. Better to state "all green, any plant material".

Hardy flowers means all kinds of hardy flowers whether from bulbs, corms, vines or herbaceous. (Hardy annual, see Annuals).

Harmony means that no one part of a design is developed at the expense of another, all elements fitting together without jarring. A unity, a consistency of likeness.

Highlight. A fine touch, a light note, a light coloured flower, leaf or grass which attracts the eye before other features in a composition.

Holder. A device for holding flowers, leaves, etc., in position in a container.

Hue is another term for colour.

Informal means a casual type of arrangement, not conventional, using a simple type of container.

Kind applies to separate genera such as roses, chrysanthemums, zinnias etc., e.g. using any kind of rose.

Line. In flower arrangement this means showing strong linear pattern or outline, using a minimum of plant material so that line is not obscured.

Mass. A massed overall design using plenty of plant material and showing no particular linear shape.

Miniature. Up to four inches is the usual overall size for a miniature arrangement. Fundamental rules of design prevail, but scale is of great importance. Tiny flowers, grasses and leaves should be used so that if magnified ten times the whole would still be in proportion. Overall size includes vase and base. State size needed.

Modern. Contrast of textures is a distinguishing feature. Modern designs are recognised by clear-cut plant forms and bold colouring. Dramatic lines are used to contrast or blend with modern decor.

Monochromatic. In colour terms this means the play on one colour using tints and shades of that particular colour. Made more interesting by introducing different textures. (See Tint Shade).

Moribana. A Japanese term to represent an arrangement in shallow container.

Niche. A space backed with cardboard, wood or other material to form a recess in which an exhibit is placed.

Nagiere. A Japanese term to represent a free or "thrown-in" style of arrangement in an upright vase.

Neutral. Grey is considered a neutral in flower colour classes. Pewter vases have a neutralising effect.

Originality. Recognised as the verve with which unusual plant material is used. An unusual vase, colour or style can produce originality.

Perennial. A plant that lives, blooms and sets seeds for more than two years.

Period. Used when exhibitors are asked to portray a particular period, such as Victorian, Georgian, *avant-garde*, modern, etc. Flowers illustrative of the period should be used.

Point system. A system of assessing the value of a flower arrangement by giving points to various principles. Not favoured by artistic judges.

Predominate. In classes where one colour or one kind of flower must predominate, this means that the particular colour or flower must be the stronger or be superior in quantity to the rest of the materials used.

Primary colours. These are red, yellow and blue.

Proportion. Similar to scale. The relationship of one part to another whether it be flowers to each other, flowers to container or the whole to background. An arrangement one foot high would be out of proportion in a three-foot niche.

Rhythm. Rhythm in a flower arrangement is usually created by the use of graduated sizes, repetition and transition without monotony, to give movement.

Receding colours. Those colours in the green, blue, violet range, so called because they appear to withdraw from vision.

Scale. See Proportion.

Secondary colours. These are orange, green and violet.

Sedges. Grass-like plant which grows in marshes or by the waterside.

Shade. Is a darker version of a colour—as maroon is to the colour red. (See frontispiece).

Space. Whether a niche is provided or not, this means the given space in which an arrangement must be placed. No exhibit should extend the given space or touch the sides of a niche.

Species. A plant form found in nature—not produced by man, as a hybrid is.

Spike. Often applied to a flower structure with very short flowers such as gladioli, antirrhinums. An unbranched single stem.

Spray. A part of a plant or shrub bearing a number of flowers on one stem such as solidago, forsythia, Michaelmas daisy, etc.

Still life. An arrangement with other objects, such as fruit, books, upturned pottery, etc., designed to make a composition or picture.

Subservient. An item (or items) less important than the others in a flower composition. It is useful as a means of relating one thing to another, but plays no important part.

Texture. The tissue structure of plant material. May be smooth or rough, dull or glossy, fine or heavy.

Tint. A lighter version of a colour, as pink is to the colour red. (See frontispiece).

Transition. The change or passage from one item to another in a flower arrangement. This is often gradual in a mass style, and good transition can give movement in a curved style.

Variations. The word variations (of one colour), allows for the use of tints and shades of a colour plus tints and shades of its analogous neighbouring colours.

Variegated. Plants marked with irregular patches of different colours. Mostly referred to in leaves bearing markings of white, cream or yellow.

Variety means a named species, hybrid or other development of a genus, such as *Achillea* Gold Plate. Achillea is the name of the hybrid plant whilst Gold Plate is the name of the variety.

Vase. A container which is taller than the diameter of the opening at the top. A word now being superseded by container.

Warm colours. Those which come in the range from yellow to red. (See frontispiece).

Water. Do not forget to put it in your container.

Wire. Wire netting used as a support should not show. Wiring of stems is not allowed.

X is for xeranthemum, a kind of annual with everlasting composite flowers.

Y is for YOU and your good efforts, which are required at every show.

Z is for ZEAL used in advancing the cause of good flower shows.

These definitions should be regarded only as a guide but, in order to meet most contingencies, I advise schedule-makers to add the words "any plant material may be used" as this covers such items as bracts, spathes (i.e. arums and anthuriums) and fungus (neither flower nor foliage) which are difficult to classify.

7

Hints for Judges

THE six main principles used in judging flower arrangements are:—

1. Interpretation of the schedule.
2. Design.
3. Colour.
4. Suitability of container to flowers.
5. Condition of plant material.
6. Distinction and originality.

Incorporated in the heading of *Design* are sections on balance, scale, harmony and rhythm, for without them there would be no good design. So before a keen flower arranger sets out to be a judge, she must be sure she understands all of the above principles. There is also a special section on table arrangements at the end of the chapter.

The National Association of Flower Arrangement Societies is doing excellent work in the training of judges, organising courses at Area level in order to give teaching and finally to assess the knowledge of those who wish to go even further, to National level.

In order to help all those wishing to try their skill at judging, and to prepare them for future examinations, I give the analysis of these main principles:

1. *Interpretation of the Schedule*

This means that the exhibit must interpret the wording of the schedule, otherwise it should not be considered further. Even if it is well designed and the flowers perfectly suited to the container, time should not be wasted on it unless the arrangement or composition exemplifies, by its shape, colour, plant material or any other factor, what is demanded of it. For instance, if the class asks for a "Gay Arrangement for a Dark Hall" and on approaching the exhibits you notice a beautiful arrangement made with mauve scabious, purple dahlias and grey foliage, you should pass it by, even if it is well designed, for you should be able to assess quickly that mauve and purple are not *gay* colours, and also that these *shades* would have no life in a *dark hall*. It is in this sort of case that your knowledge of colour will help.

A knowledge of plant material is also of great value, in fact essential to good judging; and it is used in making your first assessment of the exhibits, i.e. interpretation of schedule. If the class asks for "An Arrangement in a Basket to Illustrate Autumn Glory", you would be wrong if you gave a prize to an exhibit which featured blue delphiniums, even if it were otherwise perfect, for delphiniums would not be considered interpretative of autumn. Similarly, if a class asks for an "Arrangement of Leaves, Fruit and Flowers", make sure the exhibit contains all these three items before assessing its value in other respects. So do make sure that the exhibits you will give a second look at really do fully interpret the wording of the class before you go on to other principles.

2. *Design*

Design is of great importance. A good design has a pattern, is well scaled, has balance and rhythm. So ask yourself if the exhibit you are judging has a pattern, and do all the stems meet at a unified point? Is this point strengthened with larger or more interesting material for emphasis? Is the fine, sheer material kept to the outside or top of the design and the more dominant placed at the point where all stems meet, which is at the base of the tallest stem? Are there materials used in between the height and depth to give transition? Do your eyes travel from the outside to the centre of interest and rest there, before you assess the other points?

2a. *Scale*

This means that the flowers in the arrangement should be in scale with each other, the arrangement in scale with the vase, and the whole composition in scale with the background, space or niche which the exhibitor is allowed. Decide whether the arrangement is the right size for the container. A basic principle is that when judging an upright the flowers should be at least one and a half times higher than the height of the vase, the width each side often being two thirds of its height. An arrangement in a shallow container can be one and a half times as high as the length of the dish. These are only guides, and in advanced judging much more height is accepted, especially in a shallow dish design, where so much of the visual weight is low down. Treat the space allowed as a frame: the arrangement should fit into it with a little to spare and be neither too big or too small.

2b. *Balance*

This means that if you draw an imaginary line down through the centre of the arrangement, each side should appear visually equal. Balance can be symmetric or assymmetric. In the former the material each side of the axis can be equally distributed, in the latter, one side can be longer, but providing this long swerve is made with *fine* material and is opposed to the other side with shorter and bigger or *heavier* material, it would still appear visually balanced.

Balance can also be obtained with colour. For example, dominant colouring such as lime green, pale pink and so on, if used in large areas on the outside can over-balance a design, whereas if brought into the centre it could give stabilisation. Test your own assessment of balance by half closing your eyes, then studying your design. Imagine the central line down through your design as being the axis of a see-saw. In a symmetrical style, i.e. triangle, each side can have similar material with strength down the centre and it will appear balanced. In an asymmetrical design you can bring the weight, i.e. heavy leaves or big flowers, nearer in towards the axis on one side, and balance this at the opposing side with long fine sprays. If you assess the visual weights of the material used, it would still appear balanced, just as a man sitting near the centre of a see-saw balances a light child sitting at the end of the opposing edge.

3. *Colour*

A judge must first consider whether the colour of plant material used in the design fully interprets what is required by the schedule, e.g. yellow is cheerful and gay, blue and violet are subdued, red is exciting, green tranquil, reddish purple is royal. Certain colours are contrasting, such as nos. 1 and 7, or 3 and 10, or 6 and 12, etc. (see colour wheel frontispiece), others are analogous, some clash, some harmonise. So it all depends upon what is indicated by the class wording. Colour can express a mood, a situation or an emotion. A class for a "Gay Cocktail Party" would require some yellow in it, whereas a class expressing the mood "Dull" would require flowers or leaves of a shaded, greyish variety. Flowers, container and base should be in keeping, although if entering a class for contrasts, the container can contrast with the flowers. White is considered a colour in flower arrangement, but remember it can be too dominant when used as a container for certain flowers. White absorbs colours near to it, black throws the colours back and makes them more brilliant. In a class for "Variations of One Colour" the flowers, containers and base and/or drapes should all be in keeping. No one can state where one colour starts and another finishes, so the term variations of one colour is often of more assistance when judging than the term "An Arrangement in any One Colour". (See Tint, Shade, Variation in Definition chapter).

4. *Suitability of Container to Plant Material*

Both in colour, texture and harmony the container should suit the material it holds. Toadstools in silver is incorrect, yet toadstools in moss or wood would be in harmony. A base is considered part of the container, and it can also be the main container providing it holds a water-retaining receptacle above it. This can be a small tin or dish, but once it has been hidden it will be the base which in colour, texture or size, will be considered in conjunction with the flowers or plant material used. In period work, a container of the period being portrayed is essential. In upright designs it is better that the container is subservient, otherwise it is easy to have the eye drawn too urgently to the container. Nevertheless, in modern designs the container-cum-base can play an important part in the composition and can take a fair share in the make-up; for in modern work large spaces and contrasts are important.

5. *Condition of Plant Material*

If an arrangement possesses plant material which is not fresh then it will immediately lose points. So plants should be in good condition although the stems, blooms and shapes need not be perfect by horticultural standards. There should be no damaged or blemished plant material showing, and wiring is not encouraged. All stems should be in water or water-retaining material. A judge should not interfere with an arrangement unless she thinks the flowers are not in water, but she should have sufficient knowledge of the mechanics to see whether or not this is the case.

6. *Distinction and Originality*

This is a factor in judging that is hard to define. It can be the verve with which some unusual item, colour or container is handled. Whilst originality enters into it, the term must not be used to disguise freakishness. For instance, if some wood-stemmed leaves had been inserted all round the base of a potato and this combination were placed as focal interest, it would constitute something odd, contrived or freakish; whereas if a head of green helleborus were recessed near the wire in the centre at a point where mauve flowers protruded, it could be considered as unusually interesting. Distinction comes with some original thought, some unusual placement or combination of material. It might be an unusual placement in the niche on different sized bases which counts, or the "unthought of before" drape. Any or several of these items will lift one arrangement above the others when all other assessments are equal, and it is a point which is very important in the experience of top judging, for it may not be met lower down the scale.

TABLE-ARRANGEMENTS

Again the wording of the table should be followed. If the schedule states that the arrangement should be on a table which will seat four people, then the size of the arrangement must be taken into consideration. It is generally accepted that the size of the arrangement should be one sixth that of the table, but if only a small table can be provided, the schedule often states that the arrangement can be made to suit a table of, say, six feet long. Be careful also whether the schedule states "A Decorated Table" (in which case the exhibitor can decorate it how she likes and with one or more arrangements), or whether it states a centre piece or arrangement. Watch also whether the use of candles is allowed or whether placements or accessories are allowed, and pass the permitted number only. The colour and texture of the cloth must be considered with the whole, for the whole setting is judged and not just the centre arrangement of flowers. Remember to look for creases in cloths. Whether the table arrangement is for a luncheon, dinner, tea or a special occasion must also be considered, for gayer, more casual flowers and cloth would be used for luncheons as compared with more formal flowers for dinner, placed perhaps on a satin cloth.

HINTS FOR JUDGING

After having accepted an invitation to judge, the judge should, on receiving the schedule, read it very carefully. Should there be any ambiguous wording, she should write or phone the Show Secretary to clarify the position, making sure that the Committee, the exhibitors and the judges are all agreed on what is wanted. It is a good idea for a prospective judge to underline any particular points in the wording of the schedule which will have to be considered. For instance if there is a class for a "Cool Arrangement for a Hot Day", the word "cool" is the interpretative one and underlining it helps the judge to remember to assess the value of coolness above the other points. Also, should there be a class featuring colours, the prospective judge, by carefully reading the schedule beforehand, is given a chance to familiarise herself with aspects of colouring before she reaches the show-ground.

A judge should arrive on time and be in possession of the schedule: it is bad form to arrive, then ask for a schedule and begin to read it as if for the first time. A judge can contribute by praising the appearance of the show or by making some appreciative remark about it. The committee has usually worked very hard, so no goodwill will come of immediately pointing out improvements which could have been made with the staging etc. These suggestions can always come later in a relaxed moment. A judge should greet and be greeted by the show committee, and then ask to be left alone while she assesses the overall standard of the exhibits. A judge is seldom very sociable until after judging is finished, for in judging artistic work she has to tune in to the feeling, mood and interpretation of many exhibitors' work and cannot stop to pass the time of day to all and sundry. A judge should not waste time discussing with co-judges various exhibits which obviously do not conform to the schedule. Nothing is gained by stating how the design could have been improved. This can be done later in the judge's own time, but it must be remembered that secretaries and others are waiting on the judge's decisions, so judging should be concluded as quickly as efficiency allows.

If you are new to judging you might find it a good idea, after greeting the Show Committee, to walk round all of the classes to assess the overall standard. This allows you to tune in to the quality of the work. Then, on deciding to start to judge a certain class, walk down in front of the exhibits, noting the numbers of any which make an immediate impact on you. Condensed into this first impact will be your knowledge of the six main principles.

Having gathered, shall we say, ten which appeal to you, I suggest you go over the whole again to ascertain whether in your first enthusiasm you might have missed some which were worthy. You might now have a few more, but it is these exhibits, found on the first two runs, that you begin to judge; the rest you mentally eliminate. If you are one of two or more judges, the others should do the same, conferring all together before making final decisions.

Next try to place the first, second and third prize-winners, but do not appoint them at this stage, check first of all whether they interpret the wording of the class, and check all the other conditions. Then ask yourself how you would reply if your decision were challenged by another competitor. If you can satisfy yourself with reasons and are quite confident you are making the right decision, then, and only then, mark the card. Should you find yourself undecided between what appears two equally good designs, try starting with a maximum of 10 points and take one off for any fault such as wire showing.

The qualities of a good judge are KNOWLEDGE, FAIRNESS, EXPERIENCE, IMPARTIALITY, COURAGE and TACT, and it is in the interests of all concerned if the judge remains on hand for a while in case of queries.

JAPANESE ARRANGEMENTS

Readers might notice that I have refrained from including reference to the judging of Japanese arrangements. I have done this purposely, for when I was in Japan I found there were no set rules or principles on which these beautiful floral designs could be judged. I witnessed innumerable flower arrangement exhibitions, and although I discovered that some of the work *is* judged or assessed, so much depended on the moods and influences of the day or time that it was difficult ever to get an exact result. After grasping a principle on which to base my judgment I learned that there were several exceptions to it; and to try and adapt these principles and exceptions to English standards seems almost impossible.

Schedules in Japan are not drawn up as in Britain, and an arrangement is nearly always a personal expression. Just as it is difficult for us to appreciate the full meaning of a Japanese arrangement, so also it would not be easy for them to understand one of our Easter arrangements which featured perhaps flowers, wood, moss, coloured eggs and a china rabbit. However, rhythmic line, restraint and space should be appreciated, plus a third dimensional effect; and the ends of branches and flowers appear better if they look upwards instead of swerving downwards.

Most Japanese arrangements are seen out of competition, however, and I am sure that most experienced judges in this country who have widened their minds to all facets of the art of flower arrangement are able to assess in some measure the spiritual beauty of a Japanese arrangement and pass judgment on it if asked to do so in a competition, without trying to introduce symbolisms and exceptions to the rules.

8

The Work of Stewards

STEWARDS play an important role at all flower-arrangement shows. They should therefore fully understand the subject and be conversant with the demands of the schedule, for they are required to be on duty during staging to help exhibitors, and also to be in attendance during judging.

In the United States no competitor leaves the show room after staging without first checking with a steward to see if she has conformed to the wording of the schedule. This checking is a great aid to competitor and judge alike, for if the fault is pointed out before judging starts it avoids the judge having to place the unkind words "Not according to schedule" on the card. For instance in an "All Foliage" class, a competitor carried away by a suggestion, perhaps from another, might add a few grasses to lighten the effect, momentarily forgetting that grasses were not asked for. If this were checked with a steward the offending grasses could be pointed out and the exhibit passed ready for judging. Many have the self-discipline to keep their own check, but I have often noticed an exhibitor who is carried away by her creative ability and continues to add further plants not realising that the final items, which she thought made the arrangement, have in fact marred it.

A steward, with the aid of the show secretary, should also be aware of the number of entries in each class and where these are situated, so that she can inform the judge on arrival. She must also know how many prizes or award cards can be presented, for this is often not stated in the schedule. She must also indicate whether there are to be "best in show" awards and be most careful not to turn over any of the prizewinning cards before this has been decided. And, although she often possesses as much knowledge as the judges themselves, she MUST remain unobtrusive during judging and never offer any suggestion. It is hard, I know, but the sensibility of a judge can be completely upset by hearing a comment made by a steward, or her powers of thought can be disturbed by noise and other distractions from stewards.

Only when the class has been *completely* judged should the stewards move forward to affix the appropriate prize labels.

Nothing is more maddening to a judge who, after deciding upon the First and finding herself in the throes of deliberation over the Second and Third, is then accosted by the Steward who says—"I've found the First but where is the Second and Third?".

Judging artistic flower arrangements is no easy matter, and judging interpretative compositions very much harder still. You have only to read the chapter on judging to realise what has to be borne in a judge's mind to enable her to assess the qualities of an arrangement; and coupled with that, there is the extra emotional approach that has to be made. A judge has to "tune in", she requires being left alone in silence. So a member should not accept the position of being a steward if she thinks it entails only the sticking of labels on to cards and listening to the judges' comments. Often a judge makes no comments during judging, she is too immersed in her mental assessment, and the time for stewards to learn is after judging, when questions can be asked.

Stewards should forgive and understand if a judge appears to be unsociable during judging, for it must be remembered that she is working under a strain. When judging is finished a judge can relax, and only then is she free to exchange pleasantries with the stewards. A steward should keep away from the judge during judging, for often a judge, when nearing her decision, wishes to step quickly back to assess the effect from afar, and it is upsetting for her to step onto the steward or to have to break her train of thought by saying "Excuse me". A judge often wishes to walk up and down the rows of exhibits in order to assess the overall standard, and I advise all intending stewards not to follow in the judge's wake, for she is probably only thinking at that stage. If she is a sensitive, artistic judge, she will be trying to reach a poised level from which she can start her judging; so it will only distress her to have to worry about offending the steward at a time when she should be concentrating on the exhibits.

Stewards can and do contribute a great deal to the success of the judging, which means the success of the show. This is not an easy role to play, especially because it means subduing your own knowledge when you feel you could proffer some help. But stewards should be chosen with care, should possess knowledge and tact, should answer when spoken to without giving anything away (very difficult, this); and if there should be points in the judging which a steward has not understood she can always request a session between stewards and judges at the end of judging. I always welcome it.

9

Invitation and Exhibition

THERE comes a time when many experienced flower arrangers find themselves unable to do their best when confined to the rules of competition.

This is true of the most creative artists, for, at a certain stage of the development of their knowledge, a need is felt for freedom of expression without any hampering classifications to hold them back. Such an exhibitor needs to introduce into her work that subtle element, call it a feeling if you like, which tells her that a certain style, flower, leaf or colour is just right at that particular moment. At least just right for her, but if she has to consult the schedule to see whether its conditions leave room for her instinctive choice, then the feeling is lost. Often an artistic flower arranger will feel strongly a need to add, shall we say trails of that lovely green flower *Cobaea scandens* to an "All Green" arrangement. She knows it will look right and is convinced a better composition will result with its inclusion, yet she fears the mauve tinge on the green flowers might be viewed with suspicion by the judges, who would disqualify her design. So she does not put these attractive bellshaped flowers in, and finally makes what she considers an ordinary uninspired "All Green" arrangement.

There are hundreds of such instances, instances like the arranger who made a most inspired composition with twisted dried leaves and a *few* flowers on a rush tray with other accessories, only to discover that the schedule said "flowers must predominate"; and the other one who on finishing her arrangement felt a few grasses near the centre would lighten the effect, then discovered the schedule stated that grasses were not permitted.

Then why, you might ask, do we have competitions if there are so many who want freedom of expression, unrestricted by competition regulations? The answer is that most arrangers do not know they need the freedom until they have actually gained experience in competition. It is in competition that knowledge of technique is gained, it is here also that staging experience is learned, and by the very fact that one competitor is competing against another, the best is brought out, even latent ability is given a chance. It is this stretching a little further than we need which helps us discover ourselves, and most competitors will agree that the discipline of competitive work is really no hardship, for its mark is never lost.

There are few flower arrangers who reach the top without passing through the ranks of competitions, but as more are reaching the top, a further, less restricted, outlet must be found, in which their talent can be displayed.

We in Britain have seen many beautiful exhibitions of flower arrangements staged in private homes and other places, for charitable and various reasons, but in most of these cases the word exhibition as opposed to competition has been introduced, to attract as many entries as possible. These have not necessarily been of the highest quality for the word *exhibition* attracts those who fight shy of the idea of competition.

These exhibitions have proved an admirable source of delight to all concerned, and I applaud their inclusion in our activities; in fact I am in favour of most clubs including a non-competitive or exhibition section at their shows, for it is true that many who are encouraged in this way to exhibit, with no fear of competition, eventually discover they would *like* to compete, even if only to assess how they fare against others. This means that often one likes to start *without* competition, then if keen to move *into* competition, only to move *out* of it again, and into invitation work when all has been learned.

It is not the non-competitive beginner exhibitor that I am concerned with in this chapter, it is the top class, talented arranger who no longer wants to compete, and whose work we do not want to lose at our shows.

We must invite her, as we are now beginning to do, to show her work in invitation classes. The larger shows will, I am sure, have an invitation class in the future, so that keen members can see the work of these talented arrangers. The invited will be given freedom to do as they like, sometimes within the confines only of a niche, sometimes without. But it is in these classes that we shall eventually see some of our best work, made by artists unhampered by any restrictions who do it because they love it.

The flower club movement, and all those whose aim is to spread more beauty by the artistic use of flowers, will contribute even further by including these invitation classes in their shows, for it will afford some of our inspired arrangers a chance to introduce that extra element which has nothing to do with technical skill or rules of composition.

10

Hints on Attracting the Public to your Show

No show could be staged without the exhibitors and no exhibitor would have a chance without the show organising committee. But to make the show a success it must be patronised by members and public alike.

Publicity is of great importance, so tell everyone about your show, announcing it in excited tones first of all to your Club members. Tell them, with belief, that it is going to be a wonderful show and that with their help it can be made the talk of the town. Make them want to take part—you must not get upon the platform unless you have the ability to put across your own enthusiasm and faith to your audience.

Announce your intentions to the local Press. Give them some background stories. They may want to obtain details about the Chairman's garden for an advance story, or to learn what the oldest or youngest member is going to do at the show. They may want to hear about an unusual class and how it will be interpreted. Never mind who might be quoted in the Press, it is the show you want quoted, which in turn will draw the public which you need to make the show pay. Give some of your prominent local people or a nearby Club Chairman a complimentary ticket: it can only do good, for they in turn will talk about it. It might be a good suggestion to ask each member to sell a certain number of tickets in advance. Hand-bills are often a waste and cost money—a point to be borne in mind by small show organisers—but do get some posters out in your town, and word them in an appealing manner. Make some such statement as "The Show You Must Not Miss!", or "A Show That Will Interest All Flower Lovers!". Then add information under the headings which all journalists live by, i.e. WHEN, WHERE, WHAT, WHY and WHO? In other words you must state *when* the show will take place, *where* it will happen, *what* it is, *why* it is being staged (i.e. it could be your annual show, a summer show or a charity show), then *who* is organising it, or opening it, or any other information. State how a stranger could get to the hall—that is, by bus, train, road or underground routes. I have so often spent precious time trying to discover the whereabouts of a church hall where I am to judge, and have found that the only local reference to the show is the poster on the door of the hall. If you have chosen a theme for your show state this on the poster, for the words "A Flower Show" will no longer draw the public as being something new. You could invite them to "Come and See a Wedding in Essex", portrayed in flower arrangements by the Essex Flower Club, etc. Or you might try "The Leicester Flower Lovers' Guild invites you to an Exhibition of Flower Arrangements entitled 'This England'."

Free posters can be obtained from a number of sources such as some insurance companies and gardening magazines. *Popular Gardening* offers delightful posters of a convenient size which can be over-printed, as well as floral art diplomas. Another source could be your local art school. Ask the art master if some of the pupils would illustrate some posters for you. This could take the form of a competition for them but it would supply you with sufficient for display outside the hall and other places to get your show known in the town. The children of Club members are often talented in this respect. Do explore all avenues to obtain colourful and interesting posters. Of course the schedule, which could also act as a handbill, must be carefully and properly printed, unless the finances of the club will only allow duplicated sheets.

Once the public is in the show every endeavour should be made to keep them interested. A tombola or a raffle could be organised—do display the prizes—and a sales table will increase the takings. Sell plants and other items of interest to the flower-arranger, but do choose sales ladies who can inform and keep all enquiring visitors happy. Do tell visitors who you are. Display a small table giving information on how to join the club, also the date of your next meeting, at which visitors should be welcomed. If the membership of your club is full you might encourage visitors to form a new club and offer assistance.

If possible do promote a Tea Committee to serve teas, even if it is only a cup of tea and biscuits, it does avoid the visitor having to leave the hall for refreshment; in addition, the effort can help make profit for the show. Try to have some seating accommodation, for an art show needs to be considered and discussed, and this is far better done sitting down and relaxing.

At large shows I have found that a light background of music is a great asset, because it creates an atmosphere, so do try to provide this. But make sure the music is not a too popular hit tune, otherwise it will attract too much attention. The music should be quiet and unobtrusive.

An exchange stall is another good idea. To this members can bring any unwanted vase, gadget, accessory or base, marking it at lowest value. It can then be exchanged for any other item of similar value.

The attendance of a well-known personality

either to open the show or to present the prizes will often attract the public—do remember to mention the fact on your posters! At some larger shows, a showing of slides or a demonstration will certainly interest those who want to know how to do it themselves. It might even be possible to make an extra charge for this section of the proceedings.

A good idea is for the Committee and stewards to wear badges so that visitors know whom they may approach if wanting to ask questions. It is the day of the show that really matters: take notes on the spot of any improvements to be made the next time, but do make those who attend your show happy and interested. And smile and be happy yourself!

HAVING decided on the date of your show and booked the Hall, it is very necessary to appoint a Staging Committee composed of enthusiastic, strong members, plus husbands and sons.

Make sure enough tabling is available in the form of trestle tables for the number of entries you expect, or make sure you know where extra tables can be obtained if needed.

If you make friends with them first, a good source of supply might be the local Horticultural Society, the Red Cross, the local drill hall or church hall, schools or other organisations.

Corrugated cardboard, in many colours can be obtained, cut to requirements, from Messrs. Thomas & Easter, 23a, George Street, Baker Street, London, W.1. They also supply white and coloured lining paper for tops of tables in 12-yard rolls.

Another method of staging can be made from pieces of Essex board 3 ft. by 1½ ft. ringed together and stood up like open books. These can easily be packed and stored.

Judges' and Stewards' badges, etc. can be obtained from John Pinches Ltd., 3 Crown Buildings, Crown Street, Camberwell, London, S.E.5.

PRIZEWINNING SHOW DESIGNS

The Show Pieces illustrated on the following pages were chosen for their suitability for the season or class described.

In a number of cases photographs of prizewinning and other interesting designs were not available, and in others the names of exhibitors were not recorded. I trust that my apologies for any omissions will be accepted.

SPRING

A BREATH OF SPRING

A tall bare branch was used to obtain height in this spring design exhibited by Mrs. K. Leggett of Southgate, at one of the London and Overseas Society's Shows. Yellow daffodils were placed at the base of the tall branch—for main interest—whilst blue scillas were grouped naturally at the side of the moss-covered tree wood base. The scheme was completed by a bird's nest containing three pale blue eggs.

BUDDING SPRIN(
This rhythmic design made in a candle cup holder held by a white china model won a Firs Prize for Mrs. Perrin at the 1961 Spring Sho of the London and Overseas Flower Arrangement Society. Almond blossom was used for the fine outline swerves, whilst graduated sizes of magnolia blossom forme the main interest. Glossy green leaves gave a change of texture and the background was pal blue net.

SIMPLICIT
AN
SOPHISTICATIO
The title of this cla was amply illustrated Mrs. B. Ivory Brighton who staged t composition to wi First Prize in Lond She used graduated ar lilies in a black pli container made by hers which opposed the sim design of freesias i shell. Both were pla on a green satin b drape, the sheen of wh contrasted with dull-surfaced lil

MIXED FLOWERS

Mrs. M. McDonald of Thames Ditton, Surrey, created this beautiful prize-winning design seen at the Chelsea Flower Show. Pink striped amaryllis formed the centre of interest, placed below budded arum lilies, whilst white iris and pink roses flowed out at the sides. Young fern fronds matched the pale green of the large funkia leaves which added depth. This pink, white and pale green design was held in a black wrought-iron container.

SPRING COMPLEMENTARIES

This beautiful triangular design was created by Miss E. Shaw of Leeds, who used yellow arum lilies and lemon coloured tulips to complement the mauve and purple lilac. Leaves were introduced to give depth to the arrangement, which was backed by a pale green taffeta drape. Note the frontal flow of the lower flowers.

SPRING HARMONY

Miss P. Hankin of Cheam, Surrey, chose lemon, copper and orange colours for this scheme made in a bronze container. Orange coloured clivia surrounded by bronze double tulips formed the centre of interest at the base of the lemon coloured gladiolus, whilst paler coloured tulips flowed out at the sides. Sprays of red-orange Euphorbia fulgens *lightened the effect, whilst lachenalia, green hydrangea and freesia were also added.*

FLOWERS AND FRUIT

Using gladiolus of white colvilleii type for height, Mr. B. Halliday of Lancashire completed this flowers and fruit design with peach and flame coloured roses, carnations and gerberas intermingled with pale green nephrolepsis fern. Though faulting the rhythmic movement it won a First prize at the Southport Flower Show. The design, in addition to the edible fruit, was held on a pale-brown wooden platter.

LEEK
OPHISTICATION

Ars. I. Trevor Jones of North Wales won a First and Best in Show ith this sleek rrangement in a bronze ntainer from which ung a swathe of pleated pper-colour taffeta. Jsing bulrushes, niphofia and beige-rown Plume poppy Bocconia cordata *for eight, she placed orange ay lilies and pale green cheveria down the centre, urrounded by reversed hododendron leaves and* Begonia rex *on pposite sides.*

IN A METAL
CONTAINER

This unusual arrangement was made by Mrs. B. Plant of Leicester who used orange coloured gladiolus for height, grouping deeper orange lilies low down. Cream and flame coloured roses found their place among the light green of the fern and funkia leaves. The container was brass. Exhibited at the Royal Horticultural Society's Show at Chelsea, it was highly commended for its colouring.

LINE AND DESIGN

Miss D. Wilson of Thames Ditton, Surrey, was not afraid of space when she created this unusual design of white delphiniums variety Swan Lake to win a First Prize at the Delphinium Society's Show in London. Placed on a pin holder in a tin of water on a wooden base, the mechanics were hidden by pieces of tree wood, whilst green aspidistra leaves gave curves to the otherwise straight lines.

COOL
First Prize in this class at a London show of the National Association of Flower Arrangement Societies was won by Mr. R. Langridge of Sussex. Using all water plants, he introduced bulrushes and green iris pods for height, whilst cream primulas gave main interest. Three white water lilies floated in the water, whilst a "lizard" clambered over the stones. The dark bronze coloured container was made by the exhibitor. Apart from good balance, the effect fully interpreted the title of the class.

THE MASTER HAND

In a class for men only, Mr. D. Hurst of Surrey won a Firs[t] the National Show in London with this original design us[ing] brilliant red geraniums and variegated foliage placed besid[e] piece of twisted root wood which stood on a black block and ba

RHYTHMIC LINE

Mrs. M. E. Cole of Middlesex won a First Prize at the London N.A.F.A.S. Competition with this basket of garden flowers, using copper beech sprays for height and movement. Red-purple Jackmanii clematis *were introduced, made more obvious by the brilliant red Baccarat roses.*

AT HOME

This was the title of the class in which Mrs. E. W. Shambrook of Cheltenham entered this all-round design which featured pink roses, pink sweet peas and carnations, interspersed with sprays of grey senecio. Equally attractive on all sides, to conform with the schedule requirements, it won a First Prize at the N.A.F.A.S. Commonwealth Show.

AUTUMN

VARIETY OF ONE

In a class for the "use of only one variety of flowers, plus any other plant material", Mrs. C. Wright used graduated sizes of maroon coloured chrysanthemums for this modern design, grouped around driftwood on a wooden base. She added the maroon coloured Berberis thunbergii *for fine height, and large variegated funkia leaves for weight and depth low down.*

HARVEST HOME

Mrs. A. Gotobed made this First Prize-winning composition for the London Flower Arrangement Society in the London and Home Counties Association's inter-club contest at the Chelsea Town Hall. Using a copper preserving pan, overflowing with fruits and vegetables, for central interest, she obtained height by the use of dried astilbes and wheat with peach coloured dahlias, whilst berries, hydrangeas and pheasants' feathers were introduced here and there. Note how the height balanced the width, the colouring being emphasised by the olive-green back drape.

AUTUMN SUNSET

Peach, flame and brown were the colourings used by Mrs. P. Dean of North London to depict the above class title at the autumn show of the Floral Arrangement Association of the Home Counties. Peach coloured gladiolus and orange kniphofia formed the height whilst orange-red nerines and leaves were grouped low behind driftwood standing on a rough slice of tree wood.

HARVEST

This well designed rectangular composition backed by the lid of a market skip basket was entered in an inter-club cup contest at the London and Home Counties Show held in the Town Hall, Chelsea and perfectly illustrated the theme. Height was obtained by brown dried dock and wheat, whilst sprays of berries and shining yellow-green eleagnus leaves gave width. Berries, chrysanthemums and fruits were grouped low down with bread and a small sack of grain added for extra effect.

FESTIVAL OF HARVEST

The bronze figure of a reaper formed the centre of interest of this Harvest composition which was entered in the London and Home Counties Area Show at the Chelsea Town Hall. Added height to the wheat and the bulrushes was obtained by the use of natural coloured sacking as a backdrape, whilst beige coloured rayonnante chrysanthemums surrounded the figure low down. Pale green apples and grapes with other fruit and gourds finished the effect of this very interpretative piece.

MONOCHROMATIC

This monochromatic colour scheme illustrating the uses of tints and shades of orange was exhibited at a London show of the National Association of Flower Arrangement Societies. Pale and deep orange coloured day lilies were featured in the centre, backed by brown magnolia leaves and rust coloured pæony leaves, whilst bulrushes of a deeper shade and dried dock sprays gave a fine touch to the outline. Paler brown pine cones drooped over the edge of the brown carved wood container which stood on a brown wood base.

CHRISTMAS

CELEBRATION OF THE NATIVITY

The accessories were well placed in this composition made by Mrs. M. Lee of Whetstone to interpret the above class title at the London and Overseas Association's Christmas Show in London. Placed against a red velvet backdrape, the whitened and glittered Queen Anne's Lace gave height whilst white fresh chrysanthemums and narcissi were grouped lower down surrounded by variegated holly. The "Arum Lilies" were skeletonised magnolia leaves twisted round squirrels' tail grass to represent the spadix. The Composition gained a First Prize.

O HOLY NIGHT

This all white design placed against a midnight blue velvet background was created by Mrs. E. M. Rogers, of Chipstead, Surrey, and was seen at the Surrey County Show at Dorking. Swerves of broom and montbretia seed sprays with dried fern were used for the Hogarthian curved design. The centre was composed of various whitened seed heads all backed with whitened Magnolia grandiflora *leaves. The figurine gave spirit to the composition.*

WHITE CHRISTMAS

A white candle gave height to this mantleshelf design made by Dr. Mary Nunan of Surrey, which was shown at the National Flower Arrangement Society's Show in London. Skeletonised and whitened poppy seed heads, given false stems of wire, flowed down in front, whilst whitened datura pods and other seed heads formed central interest. Note skeletonised magnolia leaves at right which were whitened, as was all the material, to interpret the class title. A pale blue backdrape gave extra effect.

"SEE AMIDST THE WINTER'S SNOW"

Using fresh plant material, Mrs. E. Trevors made this green and snowy-white design to interpret the above class title which called for an arrangement with evergreens predominating. The base and tall piece of tree wood were covered with a snow effect, and height and width were obtained with green fir. White snowberries and other evergreens were grouped low down and highlights were obtained with a few touches of yellow winter jasmine. Seen at the Christmas Show of the Flower Arrangement Association of London and Overseas.

SCINTILLATING MINIATURES

This two-inch gilded design was made by Miss A. Mercer of Maidstone and shown among forty others at the Christmas Show of the Flower Arrangement Association of London and Overseas. Tiny fronds of adiantum fern were used as outline, whilst seed heads gold glittered formed the central interest. Fixed in a gilt container, the composition stood on a three-inch wedding-cake pedestal as was required by the class.

GREETINGS

Made by Mrs. A. Gotobed for the London and Overseas Christmas Show, this four-foot-high, red-on-white frame was completed with a curved design of whitened plant material held in plasticine wired to the frame. The outside sprays of fig were dried in a curved position, then whitened with the seed heads of cow parsley. Whitened aspidistra and mahonia were added and red glass baubles gave added life to the effect.

COMPLIMENTS OF THE SEASON

Mrs. B. Crisp of Bracknell, Berks., made this red, gold and white composition to interpret the above title at the 1961 London and Overseas Christmas Show. Using gilded berries and leaves as outline, the central "flower" was made from skeletonised magnolia leaves and was surrounded by whitened holly. All was held in a candlecup holder in a decanter filled with red water standing on a red and gold base. The red-lined greetings card held a gilded miniature arrangement.

CHRISTMAS CARD

Classes to illustrate a Christmas card attract more and more competitors each year. Here is one seen at the Royal Horticultural Society's Hall in London which shows whitened miniature plant material fixed in a red recess of this white card. The greeting was sprinkled with glitter and the red and gold bow completed the effect.

FOLIAGE

FLOWERLESS BEAUTY

A large wood burl formed the central interest in this flowerless design which was exhibited by Mrs. E. S. Evans of Southgate at the 1961 *competitions of the National Association of Flower Arrangement Societies. A twisted root and variegated flax leaves gave height whilst grey green rosettes of echeveria placed low right gave a change of form. These were opposed on the left with* Begonia rex *and funkia leaves, and it can be noted how the width of the wooden base balanced the tall central spine.*

LOVELY LEAVES

Seen at the Royal Horticultural Society's competition in London, this distinctive arrangement of leaves was created by Mrs. A. Gotobed of Hounslow, Middlesex. Using a tall bronze vase, she placed lichen-covered apple twigs for height, grouping various coloured leaves near the rim for main interest. Note how the low swerve on the right balanced the cherub on the left.

ALL FOLIAG

Mrs. M. Smith Twickenham won Fir Prize in the All Folia class at the 196 Summer Show of t National Association Flower Arrangeme Societies, with th dramatic desig A black charred branc placed in an upturn cream shell, was used f height, and the ma interest was focalised aloe plant Variegated aspidist leaves swerved out at t side and stability w established by furth black wood at the bas

THE BEAUTY OF LEAVES

A variety of colour was seen in this attractive arrangement of foliage which was in competition at the Royal Horticultural Society Hall in London. The outline of the design was composed of berberis, rosemary and other leaves, whilst shield fern and variegated ivy gave width and frontal flow. Stems of the bright red Pieris forestii *formed the centre of interest of this colourful design.*

ALL GREEN

Sprays of berberis and Grevillia robusta *formed the height and width of this First Prize-winning design made by Mrs. B. Plant of Leicester on a black wrought iron stand. Shown at the Royal Horticultural Society Hall in London, it also contained fine stems of* Lonicera nitida, *whilst flat green bergenia leaves were placed to form a frame for the heads of lighter green* Mahonia japonica *leaves which were used as focal interest.*

ALL FOLIAGE

This striking design of trimmed palmetto leaves was created by Mrs. I. Trevor Jones of North Wales and was shown at the 1961 London Show of the National Association of Flower Arrangement Societies. Tall sansevieria leaves formed a strong central spine around which the palmetto leaves were placed, whilst leaves of Fatsia japonica *gave transition from one to the other. All stood in a container placed on swirls of emerald-green pleated silk.*

THEMES

A FILM TITLE

Miranda *was the film title chosen by the late Mr. C. Oakley of Surrey who made this lovely composition to win a First Prize at the Edenbridge, Kent, Show. Using pink cactus dahlias backed by pink sea fern for main interest, he obtained height with a background of fisherman's net over turquoise-blue satin. Blue eryngiums and blue-grey echeverias and eucalyptus leaves all found their place. The figurine perched on a piece of coral was made by Mr. Oakley and placed to give continuous movement to the whole.*

NATURALISTIC STUDY

Mrs. M. Beatty made this delightful scene to win a First Prize at the British Timkin Show in Northampton. She placed a seedling ash tree beside a craglike piece of wood which stood on a wooden base covered with moss, fungus and oak twigs. A light brown carved wooden figure of a stag gave good meaning to the composition.

THE TWINS CHRISTENING

Using pink and blue flowers in a container which stood on a box backed and covered by blue and pink ninon, Mr. V. Vyner-Brooks of Southport won a special prize for this exhibit at the Ainsdale Flower Show. Blue delphiniums and pink larkspur formed the outline of the triangular design, whilst pink roses and carnations gave a change of form in the centre. Presents for both children were displayed whilst congratulatory cards and miniature storks illustrated the theme.

TINKER, TAILOR, SOLDIER, SAILOR

The above theme title allowed competitors to portray any trade or profession, and Miss E. Collis of Surrey won a First Prize with this very illustrative interpretation of "The Artist". The white frame standing on a base of grey-green satin held a design made of silver-birch bark holding a twisted branch, fungus and three pale green almonds. Outstanding in its clear-cut line, the accessories also gave spirit and meaning to this composition shown at the 1961 *London Competitions of the National Association of Flower Arrangement Societies.*

SEASCAPE

Beige rayonnante chrysanthemums bursting from the inside of a crab basket flanked by two upright pieces of driftwood were used to form this effective seascape, which was shown at the Harrogate Flower Festival. The design stood on rock slabs, and the green and white striped chlorophytum plants were placed low down between stones. A fishing net was used to give added height.

COCKTAIL BUFFET
This well designed composition seen at the Harrogate Flower Festival was created by Miss E. Shaw of Leeds. The tall sansevieria and aspidistra leaves opposed the broader leaves of Fatsia japonica *and* Begonia rex *which were placed low down in a red pottery casserole on a black iron stand. Flowers of spathiphyllum gave a highlight, whilst green glassware and colourful pottery cockerels were added as accessories.*

EATURING METAL
is was the title of a class in which Mr. George Smith of Halifax, Yorkshire ouped lemon coloured carnations and green and white variegated aspidistra leaves wing out of a bird-cage of shining brass to win a First Prize at the Harrogate ower Festival. The background was of glistening green-gold shot taffeta, but good positioning of the cage should especially be noted. Had it been stood at le level it would have been out of scale, leaving too much empty background.

GOLDEN WEDDING

Entered in the Inter-Club Competition at the London Show of the National Association of Flower Arrangement Societies; this composition illustrated a design for a "special occasion". Using flowers of gold in colour, the design was backed by green net over gold whilst champagne bottle and glasses were used as accessories. The cream and gold auratum lilies gave central interest to the gladiolus, roses and carnations.

BACCHANALIAN REVELS

Set against a green back drape, Miss E. Renny of Horsforth, Leeds, made this composition in peach and green colouring to interpret the theme class. Using gold roses with peach coloured gerberas and carnations in a gold goblet she obtained width with pale green nephrolepsis ferns. The green was repeated in the colouring of the grapes whilst further gold goblets were casually placed on the golden tray. First Prize at the Harrogate Flower Festival.

THE PANTOMIME

This pink and silver composition illustrated the pantomime of the Water Babies, and was composed of large fronds of pink dyed sea coral fern as background with pink speciosum lilies grouped low down all issuing from a large pink conch shell. The net background was misty blue and pink, and the water "bubbles" were tiny silver baubles threaded on wire. The cherub figurines completed the scene. This won a First Prize for the West Middlesex Flower Arrangement Society.

CARVED BEAUTY

This elegant looking dried arrangement made in a bronze Georgian urn by Mrs. D. Cooke of Leicester was shown at the Area Association's exhibition in London. It was composed of brown dried artichokes and brown-glycerine-preserved Garrya elliptica *and camellia leaves. Good balance was obtained by placement at the right of the marble base, whilst an extra artichoke was used to complete the line.*

DRY BUT NOT DULL

A rough wood base held this interesting dry design made by Miss P. Burdett of Edgware, seen at the London and Home Counties Show at the Chelsea Town Hall. Dry eucalyptus seed sprays formed the height whilst large cones gave central interest. Glycerine-preserved magnolia leaves formed a background to a number of dried mushrooms impaled on sticks, cleverly placed running down to and through the cones.

SUMMER'S ECHO

A certain natural charm is obvious in this dry arrangement on a wooden base. Sprays of beech nut gave height whilst large pieces of cream and tan coloured fungus formed the main interest at the base of the upright wood. Dry dock, twigs and glycerine-preserved ivy leaves were added low down. This won a Second Prize at Chelsea Town Hall.

STUDY IN BROWN

Different varieties of pine cones formed the main interest in this dry design made in a wooden container standing on two polished wooden bases. Tall seed sprays and poppy seed heads formed a rhythmic movement through the composition swerving off to the two cedar cones placed at the left. This was arranged by Dr. Mary Nunan of Surrey and exhibited at one of the London Flower Arrangement Society's shows.

WINTER'S APPROACH

This coned larch spray simulating a bare tree was placed behind a large burl of wood on a base, the curves of which made an enchanting hide-away for the tiny model mice. This appealing composition was shown at one of the London Flower Arrangement Society's shows and won a prize for the exhibitor, whose name is not traceable.

FRAMED

This monochromatic study of dried plant material in a frame was made and shown by Mrs. L. Egerton-Bird of Weymouth, Dorset. Composed in muted shades of soft green, bronze, orange and beige, it was made up of poppy, love-in-the-mist and montbretia seed heads, varnished cupressus and teazles with Lagurus ovatus, Briza maxima *and pampas grasses. Bleached* Ruscus aculeatus *gave highlights near the centre pine cones. Slightly reminiscent of a Grinling Gibbons carving, it was mounted in cement on reversed hardboard.*

JAPANESE

MODERN
Mrs. M. E. Cole of Kenton, Middlesex, created this modern Japanese design which featured three orange coloured Strelitzia reginae *blooms placed in an upturned glazed container standing on a wooden base. Ivy berries, leaves and root wood were placed at a unifying point. Note the upward look of the flowers.*

NAGIERE

A twisted twig of oak gave rhythmic line to this lovely Nagiere (upright) arrangement created by Miss P. Hankin of Surrey in a tubular bamboo container standing on two black wooden bases. Two pink Speciosum lilies, one flowing more forward than the other, added a touch of colour to this restrained design. Note the value of space which accents the line.

MORIBANA

This beautiful Moribana (shallow container) arrangement was made by Mrs. J. Dewar of Northwood, Middlesex, in a suna-bachi bronze container. Twisted ivy root sprays, carefully trimmed, gave height and linear space to this arrangement which was completed with two heads of pink rhododendron. Note how the lower flower protrudes forward over the stones which glisten through the water, the second flower being recessed to add a three-dimensional effect.

ONE AND ONE

A hollow piece of tree wood gave height and balanced this design made by Mrs. J. Ginns of Welwyn Garden City. The wood framed the single white iris which rose from the shallow dish made by the exhibitor. The water lily placed on a separate kenzan at the right completed the divided arrangement often known as divided kenzan style or one and one, since two is considered unlucky in Japan.

CLASSICAL

This appealing arrangement made by Mrs. A. Gotobed in a classical Hanaike bronze container was composed of trimmed pine branches and three yellow double tulips skilfully placed. Japanese women spend hours trimming branches; this is said to aid repose. Note the upward turn of the flowers.

FREE STYLE

This moribana arrangement, using two pink gladiolus with pale green asparagus fern, was made by Miss Stella Coe of the Sogetsu school. Full of restraint, the flowers were held on a holder in a modern pink tinged grey pottery container which stood on a black scroll base.

TABLES

COOL FOR SUMMER

Celadon green satin cloth formed the basis of this green and white table setting which won First Prize for the West Hampshire Floral Arrangement Society at the 1961 competitions of the National Association of Flower Arrangement Societies, held in the Royal Horticultural Society's Halls, London. The candle cups of the glittering crystal drop candelabra were filled with white Colvilleii gladiolus, roses and freesias, whilst trails of green and white tradescantia and leaves of maranta united the whole. This centrepiece was flanked on each side by two crystal drop candlesticks holding similar flowers.

FOR A SUMMER EVENING
Set on a sheet of green glass this white and green table setting was made by Mrs. V. Gardner and Mrs. A. Strachan for the Surrey Floral Decoration Society at the National Association of Flower Arrangement Society's 1961 competition in London. Fine white Colvilleii gladiolus gave height behind the figurine whilst lemon coloured roses and leaves gave depth low down. Lemons, pale green grapes and roses were grouped in front of the figure, the whole scheme echoing the colouring of the plates.

HARVESTERS' LUNCH

This was the unusual title of a class at the Delphinium Society's Show in London, for the stately delphinium is not as a rule associated with Harvest. However, Miss E. Hambly Parker of Hemel Hempstead treated this rather formal flower in such a manner as to win a First Prize. Using green-blue delphiniums, she added green tinged oats and wheat low down whilst creamy white wild cow parsley was placed bursting out of the flat basket. The accessories added colour and meaning to the title of the class.

FORMALITY

Mrs. J. Denham Davis of Hookwood, Surrey, made this beautiful red and pale blue table setting to win a First Prize at the Christmas Show of the National Association of Flower Arrangement Societies. The centrepiece was composed of red gladiolus, sprays of red berries and carnations, whilst rosy red apples and purply red grapes were poised each side to give an all round effect. The cloth was pale blue, the napkins red on blue glass plates, whilst the candles were red in ormulu gilt candlesticks. Matching blue cigarettes were placed beside blue containers filled with red tipped matches.

STAGING

THE ENTRANCE

It is a good idea to put visitors in the mood for what they are to see, so posters and decorations should be placed to spell a welcome either in the entrance hall or even outside it. Here using peach, cream and pale green flowers and leaves, three members of the Surrey Floral Decoration Society decorated the entrance to the charity exhibition staged at the Putney Hospital for Incurables.

THE PLATFORM

This table, placed in the centre of a platform, was decorated as for Harvest Supper at the Harvest Home Show, staged by the London and Home Counties Floral Arrangement Association in the Chelsea Town Hall. The large central arrangement was flanked each side by groupings of fruit, all on a scarlet cloth, whilst the front draping was covered with dry groupings of pampas grass and vegetables, as well as specially baked bread.

A SIDE WALL

Still life with fruit and foliage was portrayed by the Rugby Flower Club for the Midlands Area Association to complete this side wall at the combined Area Associations' Show in London. Colourful fruits, green leaves, pewter and green glass on rush mats, backed by netting, made up the setting.

ALL SET FOR VIEWING

The new Hall of the Royal Horticultural Society in London as seen set with corrugated cardboard niches for the first Flower Arrangement Academy staged in 1952 by the Dorset, Leicester, London and Colchester Flower Decoration Societies. Note how the low tables down the centre emphasised the vista to the end of the Hall where pedestals were staged.